Lingo Dingo
and the
German astronaut

Written by Mark Pallis
Illustrated by James Cottell

For my awesome sons Oscar and Felix- MP

For Sophia - JC

LINGO DINGO AND THE GERMAN ASTRONAUT

Story edited by Natascha Biebow, Blue Elephant Storyshaping
First Printing, 2021
ISBN: 978-1-913595-86-9
NeuWestendPress.com

Lingo Dingo
and the
German astronaut

Written by Mark Pallis

Illustrated by James Cottell

NEU WESTEND
— PRESS —

This is Lingo. She's a Dingo and she loves helping.
Anyone. Anytime. Anyhow.

It was a big day.

Lingo's friend, Sue, was off on a mission to the International Space Station. Departure was in one minute and Sue was running late.

"Look out for the banana skin!" cried Lingo.

"I'll be OK, but the mission is over," said Sue.

"I can help!" said Lingo.

But there were only thirty
seconds to launch:
hurry Lingo!

Quick as a shooting star, Lingo climbed up into the rocket.

"Don't forget this. It's a battery for the Space Station," said Sue.

The countdown began: Five, four...

Lingo buckled up.

3...

She felt nervous.

2...

1...

Blast off!

Lingo soon arrived at the International Space Station.

She was in space and she could f l o a t !

"Willkommen!" said an astronaut. "Mein Name ist Rex. Ich bin Astronaut." Lingo tried a reply in German, "Mein Name ist Lingo."

Willkommen = Welcome; **Mein Name ist** = My name is
Ich bin Astronaut = I am an astronaut

"Komm mit," said Rex. He led Lingo around the Space station.

"Die Toilette."

"Das Labor."

"Das Schlafzimmer. Und mein Teddybär."

Komm mit = follow me; Die Toilette = the toilet; Das Labor = the laboratory
Das Schlafzimmer = the bedroom; Und mein Teddybär = and my teddybear

Suddenly a BEEPING blared out!

"Hast du die neue Batterie dabei?" asked Rex.

Lingo wasn't sure what 'Batterie' meant. She checked her pockets.

Hast du die neue Batterie dabei? = have you got the new battery?
Batterie = battery

Eine Angelrute = a fishing rod; Nein = no
Eine Kamera = a camera; Ja = yes; Raumanzüge anziehen! = space suits on!

"Drehe ihn nach links," said Rex, pointing to the handle.

Lingo turned it right. "Nicht nach rechts, nach links!" cried Rex. Lingo turned it left and the hatch swung open.

rechts = right; **links** = left
Nicht nach rechts, nach links = not to the right, to the left

Space was waiting for them!
They got straight to work changing the battery.
"Reiche mir bitte den Schraubendreher," said Rex.

Lingo passed Rex the screwdriver and he
screwed the new battery into place.

Schraubendreher = screwdriver; **bitte** = please
Reiche mir bitte den Schraubendreher = pass me the screwdriver

"Geschafft! Gib mir fünf," he said.

Lingo realised Rex wanted
a high five.

Success!

Lingo called Sue with the good news:

Geschafft = We did it
Gib mir fünf = give me five

The view was incredible.

Rex pointed out all the things to see.

"Die Sonne."

"Die Erde."

Die Erde = the earth; **Die Sonne** = the sun

But Lingo spotted something else ...!

Die Sterne = the stars; **Der Mond** = the moon; **Der Roboterarm** = the robotic arm

"Mein Teddy!" cried Rex.

Rex's teddy must have floated out of the airlock.

"Benutze den Roboterarm," he said.

Lingo was going to use the robotic arm.

Mein Teddy = my teddy
Benutze den Roboterarm = use the robotic arm

Rex called out the directions: "Rauf. Runter.
Du hast ihn fast. Greifen!"

Lingo closed the hand...

but Teddy was too far away!

"Nein! Teddy ist verloren," cried Rex.

"I can help," said Lingo.

She noticed something
else floating nearby.

Her fishing rod!

Lingo swung the hook.

Ich drücke die Daumen = Fingers crossed

"Ich drücke die Daumen," said Rex.
The hook caught Teddy's bow tie!

"Mein Freund," cheered Rex.
"Partyzeit."

Mein Freund = my friend; **Partyzeit** = let's celebrate

Rex pressed a button and funky music boomed out.

Time to bust some zero gravity dance moves

"Ich tanze, du tanzt, Teddy tanzt,
wir tanzen!" laughed Rex.

Ich tanze = I dance; **du tanzt** = you dance
Teddy tanzt = teddy dances; **wir tanzen** = we dance

"Wo ist das Vögelchen?" said Rex, and took a photo.

Wo ist das Vögelchen? = Where is the birdie? / Say cheese!

"Hast du Durst?" asked Rex. He squeezed big blobs of water over to Lingo. "Das ist Wasser," he said. "Bist du hungrig?" asked Rex.

Hast du Durst? = are you thirsty?; **Das ist Wasser** = that is water
Bist du hungrig? = are you hungry?

'Hungrig' must mean 'hungry' thought Lingo. "Yes," she replied. "Ich auch," Rex agreed.

It was time for space ice cream: "Eiscreme!" he said.

Ich auch = me too; **Eiscreme** = ice cream

Lingo and Rex snuggled into bed.
What an incredible day.

"Ich liebe den Weltraum," said Rex.
"Yes," agreed Lingo. "Ich auch."
"Schlaf gut, Lingo," said Rex.

Ich liebe = I love; **den Weltraum** = space

Lingo didn't have time to wonder what "Schlaf gut" meant, she was already fast asleep.

Schlaf gut = sleep well

Learning to love languages

An additional language opens a child's mind, broadens their horizons and enriches their emotional life. Research has shown that the time between a child's birth and their sixth or seventh birthday is a "golden period" when they are most receptive to new languages. This is because they have an in-built ability to distinguish the sounds they hear and make sense of them. The Story-powered Language Learning Method taps into these natural abilities.

How the Story-powered language learning Method works

We create an emotionally engaging and funny story for children and adults to enjoy together, just like any other picture book. Studies show that social interaction, like enjoying a book together, is critical in language learning.

Through the story, we introduce a relatable character who speaks only in the new language. This helps build empathy and a positive attitude towards people who speak different languages. These are both important aspects in laying the foundations for lasting language acquisition in a child's life.

As the story progresses, the child naturally works with the characters to discover the meanings of a wide range of fun new words. Strategic use of humour ensures that this subconscious learning is rewarded with laughter; the child feels good and the first seeds of a lifelong love of languages are sown.

For more information and free learning resources visit www.neuwestendpress.com

You can learn more words and phrases with these hilarious, heartwarming stories from **NEU WESTEND** — PRESS —

LEARN 50 GERMAN WORDS
THE FABULOUS LOST & FOUND
AND THE LITTLE GERMAN MOUSE
WRITTEN BY MARK PALLIS
ILLUSTRATED BY PETER BRYNTON
NEU WESTEND PRESS

NEU WESTEND PRESS

LINGO DINGO
and the German chef
Written by Mark Pallis
Illustrated by James Cottell

Makes learning German easy and fun!

Learn 50 German words

@MARK_PALLIS on twitter
www.neuwestendpress.com

To download your FREE certifcate, and more cool stuff, visit
www.neuwestendpress.com

@jamescottell on INSTAGRAM
www.jamescottellstudios.com

> "I want people to be so busy laughing, they don't realise they're learning!"
>
> Mark Pallis

Crab and Whale is the bestselling story of how a little Crab helps a big Whale. It's carefully designed to help even the most energetic children find a moment of calm and focus. It also includes a special mindful breathing exercise and affirmation for children.
Also available in French, Italian, German & Spanish!
Featured as one of Mindful.org's
'Seven Mindful Children's books'

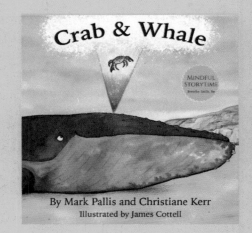

Do you call them hugs or cuddles?

In this funny, heartwarming story, you will laugh out loud as two loveable gibbons try to figure out if a hug is better than a cuddle and, in the process, learn how to get along.

A perfect story for anyone who loves a hug (or a cuddle!)

www.markpallis.com

Printed in Great Britain
by Amazon